Second Edition

Learning World ③ WORKBOOK

Listening Homework

pp.45～54はCDを聞きながら答えるリスニングテストです。

問題は英検5級レベルに対応しています。

音声はCD番号で頭出しができ、2回ずつくり返されます。

なお、英検では、次の問題までの時間の間隔は10秒ですが、このCDでは7秒になっています。

Let's try. は英検5級対応問題です。ユニットごとに4週目に配置しました。
The "Let's try." pages are modelled on STEP test level 5 questions.

Listening Homework　pp.45～54は英検5級レベルのリスニング問題です。英検対策として、付属のCDを聞いて解きましょう。

何題できたかな？

Listening Homework ❶	Listening Homework ❷	Listening Homework ❸	Listening Homework ❹	Listening Homework ❺	Listening Homework ❻	Listening Homework ❼	Listening Homework ❽	Listening Homework ❾	Listening Homework ❿
/8	/8	/8	/8	/8	/8	/8	/8	/8	/8
Date　·	Date　·	Date　·	Date　·	Date　·	Date　·	Date　·	Date　·	Date　·	Date　·

書き順に決まりはありません。
この書き順は1つの例です。

ordinal numbers	12 months	days of the week
1st first		
2nd second		
3rd third		
4th fourth		
5th fifth		
6th sixth		
7th seventh		
8th eighth		
9th ninth		
10th tenth		
11th eleventh		
12th twelfth		

Monday   January
February
Tuesday
October
Sunday
March
November
December
Friday
Saturday
August
September
April
Thursday
July
May
Wednesday
June

1 Write your own answers.

1 I have _____

2 I don't have _____

3 I want _____

4 I don't want _____

5 I like _____

6 I don't like _____

2 Words

1 moon
( ) _____

2 sky
( ) _____

3 mountain
( ) _____

4 hill
( ) _____

5 flower
( ) _____

6 lake
( ) _____

7 cloud
( ) _____

8 star
( ) _____

2

1 Write your own answers.

1 What is your name?

_____

_____

2 What is your family name?

_____

_____

3 How old are you?

_____

_____

4 Where do you live?

_____

_____

5 What is the date today?

_____

_____

6 What day of the week is it today?

_____

_____

7 When is your birthday?

_____

_____

2 Words

1 third ( ) _____		**2** second ( ) _____	
3 family name ( ) _____		**4** elementary school ( ) _____	
5 grade ( ) _____		**6** sunny ( ) _____	
7 April ( ) _____		**8** January ( ) _____	

1 Find the correct English and write the answers.

❶ 答えを知らないときは？

_____
_____
_____

❷ 質問の意味がわからないときは？

_____
_____
_____

❸ もっとゆっくり話してほしいときは？

_____
_____
_____

❹ catの書き方を聞くときは？

_____
_____
_____

❺ 作業ができたときは？

_____
_____
_____

❻ 英語でなんと言うかがわからないときは？

_____
_____
_____

I'm finished.	I don't know.
More slowly, please.	How do you say … in English?
How do you spell 'cat'?	I don't understand.

2 words

❶ firefighter ( )		❷ taxi driver ( )	
❸ student ( )		❹ family ( )	
❺ introduce ( )		❻ understand ( )	
❼ say ( )		❽ slowly ( )	

Choose and write the correct answers.

1 I ＿＿＿＿＿＿ eleven years old.

     ❶ can   ❷ like   ❸ am   ❹ is

2 I am ＿＿＿＿＿＿ the fifth grade.

     ❶ in   ❷ at   ❸ from   ❹ go

3 My father ＿＿＿＿＿＿ a taxi driver.

     ❶ like   ❷ he   ❸ am   ❹ is

4 ＿＿＿＿＿＿ is your name?

     ❶ Where   ❷ What   ❸ How   ❹ My

5 You ＿＿＿＿＿＿ my teacher.

     ❶ is   ❷ are   ❸ can   ❹ have

6 Shota and I ＿＿＿＿＿＿ good friends.

     ❶ is   ❷ are   ❸ live   ❹ am

7 I ＿＿＿＿＿＿ glad to meet you.

     ❶ is   ❷ are   ❸ am   ❹ have

8 **A:** Do you like dogs?   **B:** No, I ＿＿＿＿＿＿.

     ❶ like   ❷ do   ❸ don't   ❹ dogs

9 **A:** Can you ski?   **B:** Yes, ＿＿＿＿＿＿ can.

     ❶ you   ❷ can   ❸ ski   ❹ I

10 **A:** Do you know Mr. Tanaka?   **B:** Yes, I ＿＿＿＿＿＿. He is Maki's father.

     ❶ do   ❷ know   ❸ is   ❹ Mr. Tanaka

1 Circle the correct answers and write the sentences.

1 He (is   isn't) a dentist.

_____
_____
_____

2 Is he a teacher?   Yes, he (is   do   isn't).

_____
_____
_____

3 She (is   isn't) a doctor.

_____
_____
_____

4 What is she? (Yes, she is.   No, she isn't.   She is a teacher.)

_____
_____
_____

5 She (is   isn't) a scientist.

_____
_____
_____

6 What is she? (Her name is Mrs. Sato.   She is a scientist.)

_____
_____
_____

2 words

1 police officer ( )		2 engineer ( )	
3 carpenter ( )		4 farmer ( )	
5 fisherman ( )		6 nurse ( )	
7 brave ( )		8 strong ( )	

1 Write the questions and answers.

1

Q What is she doing?

A She is reading.

2

Q _____

A _____

3

Q _____

A _____

4

Q _____

A _____

5

Q _____

A _____

6

Q _____

A _____

sleeping   cleaning   crying   cooking   reading   running

2 Words

1 cleaning ( ) _____		**2** crying ( ) _____	
3 practicing ( ) _____		**4** driving ( ) _____	
5 listening to … ( ) _____		**6** talking with … ( ) _____	
7 waiting for … ( ) _____		**8** busy ( ) _____	

1 Find and write the correct English expression for each sign.

1 さわる べからず

2 従業員専用 (の入口)

3 芝生に入る べからず

4 横断禁止

5 行き止まり

6 一方通行

7 引く

8 非常口

9 故障中

10 閉店

11 左側通行

12 ここで お待ちください

Staff Only	Closed	Hands Off	One Way
Keep Off the Grass	Fire Exit	Do Not Cross	Dead End
Pull	Wait Here	Keep Left	Out Of Order

2 words

❶ make my bed
( )

❷ eat more slowly
( )

❸ go to bed
( )

❹ go out
( )

❺ jump around
( )

❻ make noise
( )

❼ stay up late
( )

❽ yell
( )

Let's try. 2

Choose and write the correct answers.

① _____ do you live?

    ❶ How   ❷ What   ❸ Where   ❹ When

② _____ is your birthday?

    ❶ How   ❷ What   ❸ Where   ❹ When

③ _____ is your name?

    ❶ What   ❷ How   ❸ Do   ❹ When

④ Mark is _____ to music in his room.

    ❶ getting   ❷ reading   ❸ writing   ❹ listening

⑤ My mother is _____ dinner in the kitchen.

    ❶ reading   ❷ cooking   ❸ running   ❹ playing

⑥ What _____ do you get up in the morning?

    ❶ time   ❷ day   ❸ clock   ❹ week

⑦ I go to school _____ foot.

    ❶ by   ❷ on   ❸ under   ❹ in

⑧ Good-bye. _____ you next week.

    ❶ Go   ❷ Play   ❸ Do   ❹ See

⑨ _____ bag is this? It's my bag.

    ❶ Where   ❷ Who   ❸ Whose   ❹ Can

⑩ _____ I come in? Of course.

    ❶ What   ❷ May   ❸ Do   ❹ Am

1 Write the English and read aloud.

1. _a dog_ | _dogs_

2. _____ | _____

3. _____ | _____

4. _____ | _____

5. _____ | _____

6. _____ | _____

2 Complete the pictures. Write the answers.

1. Three boxes. Draw one cat in each box.

   How many cats? _____ cats

2. Four dogs. Draw four dots on each dog.

   How many dots? _____ dots

3. Three tables. Draw five oranges on each table.

   How many oranges? _____ oranges

4. Five plates. Draw two fish on each plate.

   How many fish? _____ fish

1 Copy each word and read aloud.

a woman | women

a man | men

a child | children

2 Answer the questions.

1 How many days are there in a week? _____ days

2 How many hours are there in a day? _____ hours

3 How many minutes are there in one hour? _____ minutes

4 How many boys are there in the class? _____ boys

5 How many girls are there in the class? _____ girls

3 words

1 farm (   )

2 barn (   )

3 turkey (   )

4 chick (   )

5 on (   )

6 in (   )

7 in front of (   )

8 between (   )

1 **Answer the questions.**

mouse　cow　tiger　rabbit　dragon　snake　horse　sheep　monkey　rooster　dog　wild boar

1 What is between the mouse and the tiger?

_____ is _____

2 What is between the snake and the sheep?

3 What is between the monkey and the dog?

4 What is between the dragon and the horse?

5 What is between the rooster and the wild boar?

6 What is between the cow and the rabbit?

7 What is between the dog and the mouse?

2 **Words**

1 yours (　　　)

2 mine (　　　)

3 which one (　　　)

4 parking lot (　　　)

5 that one (　　　)

6 wild boar (　　　)

7 rooster (　　　)

8 dragon (　　　)

Choose and write the correct answers.

1
A How _____ sisters do you have?
B I have one sister.

❶ much ❷ three
❸ many ❹ time

2
A How _____ is this doll?
B It is 10 dollars.

❶ much ❷ there
❸ many ❹ time

3
A _____ your mother busy today?
B Yes, she is.

❶ Am ❷ Is
❸ Are ❹ What

4
A _____ play catch.
B Yes, let's.

❶ Do ❷ Let's
❸ What ❹ On

5
I _____ to bed at ten o'clock.

❶ go ❷ take
❸ have ❹ want

6
My brother is _____ his shirt.

❶ cooking
❷ washing
❸ swimming
❹ running

7
There are _____ months in a year.

❶ six
❷ twelve
❸ January
❹ ten

8
A Do you have any brothers?
B Yes, _____ do.

❶ I ❷ he ❸ you
❹ my brother

9
A What _____ is it now?
B It Is four thirty.

❶ weather ❷ day
❸ time ❹ o'clock

10
A When do you play soccer?
B I play soccer _____ school.

❶ on ❷ after
❸ under ❹ to

1 Choose the correct picture and write the alphabet. Write your own answers.

1 Can you dive into water? ☐

2 Can you play basketball? ☐

3 Can you score a basket? ☐

4 Can you score a goal? ☐

5 Can you bake a cake? ☐

6 Can you ride a unicycle? ☐

Ⓐ Ⓑ Ⓒ Ⓓ Ⓔ Ⓕ

2 Write the Japanese in the ( ) under each picture.

3 Fill in the blanks with can or can't.

1 A penguin _____ fly in the sky.

2 A snake _____ swim in the water.

3 A panda _____ climb a tree.

4 A rooster _____ lay eggs.

1 **Put the words in the correct order and complete the sentences.**

1 This _____

| my | wheelchair | is | . |

2 I _____

| am | my | family | of | proud | . |

3 He _____

| play | soccer | , | can | too | . |

4 He _____

| a | is | athlete | great | . |

5 Can _____

| read | you | Braille | ? |

6 I _____

| with | can | everywhere | him | go | . |

2 words ··

1 be proud of	**2** wheelchair
( ) _____	( ) _____
3 great	**4** athlete
( ) _____	( ) _____
5 guide dog	**6** everywhere
( ) _____	( ) _____
7 smart	**8** Braille
( ) _____	( ) _____

1 **Fill in the blanks with someone's name.**

① _____ can speak English very well.

② _____ can speak English a little.

③ _____ can't speak English at all.

④ _____ can play the piano very well.

⑤ _____ can play the piano a little.

⑥ _____ can play the recorder very well.

⑦ _____ can sing very well.

2 words ....

❶ speak _____ ( ) _____	❷ well _____ ( ) _____
❸ very well _____ ( ) _____	❹ a little _____ ( ) _____
❺ not … at all _____ ( ) _____	❻ of course _____ ( ) _____
❼ recorder _____ ( ) _____	❽ write _____ ( ) _____

Let's try 4

Choose and write the correct answers.

① December is the _____ month of the year.

     ❶ ninth   ❷ first   ❸ summer   ❹ twelfth

② I like _____ science books.

     ❶ reading   ❷ playing   ❸ going   ❹ speaking

③ My mother goes to work _____ train.

     ❶ for   ❷ by   ❸ on   ❹ to

④ Welcome _____ my home!

     ❶ on   ❷ to   ❸ in   ❹ under

⑤ My bag is old. I want a new _____.

     ❶ big   ❷ two   ❸ one   ❹ old

⑥ I have _____ study tonight.

     ❶ don't   ❷ to   ❸ like   ❹ on

⑦ Keiko and I are good friends. _____ like tennis.

     ❶ They   ❷ You   ❸ We   ❹ She

⑧ Mr. Smith is our English teacher. He is _____ England.

     ❶ an   ❷ likes   ❸ from   ❹ on

⑨ Thank you _____ the present.

     ❶ for   ❷ You're welcome.   ❸ nice   ❹ on

⑩ I am thirsty. I want something _____ drink.

     ❶ for   ❷ on   ❸ under   ❹ to

$\begin{pmatrix} I \\ You \end{pmatrix}$ **have** a dog.   ➡ $\begin{pmatrix} He \\ She \end{pmatrix}$ **has** a dog.

1 Write the Japanese and fill in the blanks.

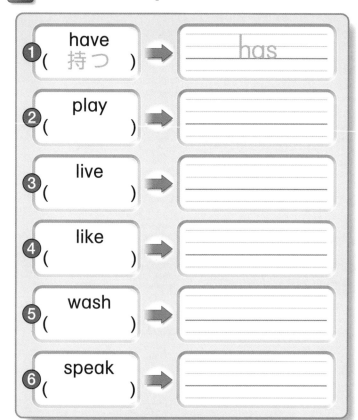

1 have (持つ) ➡ has

2 play ( ) ➡ _____

3 live ( ) ➡ _____

4 like ( ) ➡ _____

5 wash ( ) ➡ _____

6 speak ( ) ➡ _____

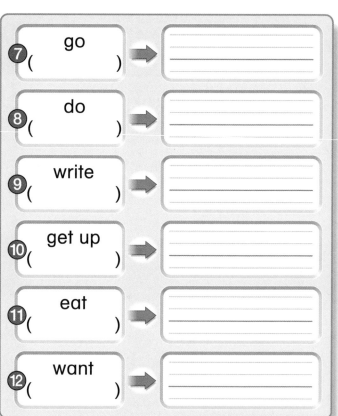

7 go ( ) ➡ _____

8 do ( ) ➡ _____

9 write ( ) ➡ _____

10 get up ( ) ➡ _____

11 eat ( ) ➡ _____

12 want ( ) ➡ _____

2 Read and fill in the blanks.

 I   my brother

1 I have a sister.   My brother _____ two sisters.

2 I live in Denver.   My brother _____ in Denver, too.

3 I play tennis.   My brother _____ tennis, too.

4 I want a new racket.   My brother _____ a new racket, too.

5 I get up at seven o'clock in the morning.   My brother _____ up at seven o'clock, too.

6 I go to school by bike.   My brother _____ to school by bike, too.

1 Write in **do** or **does**.

1

_____ you like milk?

Yes, I _____ .

2

I _____ not like coffee.

3

My sister _____ not like milk.

4

_____ your mother play tennis?

No, she _____ not.

5

When _____ you play tennis?

6

Where _____ you and your sister live?

2 Describe a kangaroo.

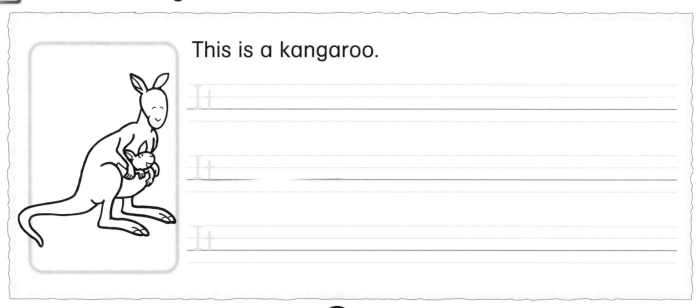

This is a kangaroo.

_____

_____

_____

1 **Who does what in your family?**

In my family,

2 **Write your own answers.**

① Who teaches English?

② Who teaches music?

③ Who teaches Japanese?

3 **Words** ·······································

❶ always ( )	❷ sometimes ( )
❸ never ( )	❹ clean your room ( )
❺ wash the dishes ( )	❻ feed the pet ( )
❼ buy groceries ( )	❽ clean the bathroom ( )

Choose and write the correct answers.

1

A This is a present for you.

B Wow! _____

❶Hello.　　❷You're welcome.　　❸Thank you.　　❹Here you are.

2

A Let's go on a hike.

B _____

❶Yes, let's.　　❷Yes, I do.　　❸I'm fine.　　❹On foot.

3

A May I speak to Tom, please?

B _____

❶He is fine.　❷This is Tom speaking.　❸Tom is not speaking.　❹Thank you.

4

A Where are you going?

B _____

❶To school.　❷With my friends.　❸At seven o'clock.　❹On foot.

5

A Do you want a new video game?

B _____

❶No, you don't.　❷That's a video game.　❸Yes, I do.　❹Yes, it is.

6

A How is the weather today?

B _____

❶Sunny and hot.　❷Thank you.　❸In the morning.　❹Yes, please.

7

A Where are you, Dad?

B _____

❶I am sleeping.　❷I am in the kitchen.　❸I am fine.　❹He is in the kitchen.

1 Write the questions and answers.

you

1. do your homework

Q Do you have to do your homework?
A Yes, I do. I have to

2. cook dinner

Q
A

3. go to *juku*

Q
A

your teacher

4. do her homework

Q Does your teacher have to do her homework?
A No, she doesn't. She doesn't have to

5. cook dinner

Q
A

6. go to *juku*

Q
A

2 words

1 have to
( )

2 right now
( )

3 stop talking
( )

4 stop laughing
( )

5 stop running
( )

6 stop writing
( )

7 stop watching
( )

8 stop playing
( )

❷

Find the correct adjective. Write the word under each picture.

① （ハンサムな）

② （きたない）

③ （うるさい）

④ （つかれている）

⑤ （活発な）

⑥ （小心の）

⑦ （正直な）

⑧ （美しい）

⑨ （よくちらかす）

⑩ （こわい）

⑪ （かわいい）

⑫ （かっこいい）

⑬ （ゆうかんな）

⑭ （お金持ちの）

⑮ （年をとっている）　89歳

⑯ （若い）　14歳

⑰ （失礼な）

⑱ （しんせつな）　Thank you very much.

⑲ （ねむい）

⑳ （偉大な）

cheerful	handsome	young	scary	cool	beautiful
dirty	kind	rude	old	rich	timid	sleepy
pretty	brave	noisy	tired	great	honest	messy

1 Look at the picture and complete the sentences.

the Matterhorn	Mt. Fuji	Mt. McKinley	Mt. Everest
(4,477m)	(3,776m)	(6,194m)	(8,848m)

9,000 / 8,000 / 7,000 / 6,000 / 5,000 / 4,000 / 3,000 / 2,000 / 1,000 / 0

Which mountain is higher?

① _____ is higher than _____

②

③

④ _____ is the highest.

2 Words

① taller ( )
② stronger ( )
③ shorter ( )
④ longer ( )
⑤ bigger ( )
⑥ smaller ( )
⑦ better ( )
⑧ worse ( )

Let's try. 6

Choose and write the correct answers.

1
A How old is this building?

B _____

1 It is old.
2 It is one hundred years old.
3 He is five years old.
4 It is a city hall.

2
A How are you?

B Fine, thank you. _____

1 Do you?
2 And you?
3 I'm fine.
4 Yes, I am.

3
A Pass me the sugar, please.

B _____

1 You're welcome.
2 It is mine.
3 Here you are.
4 Yes, I do.

4
A Does Santa Claus come to your house?

B _____

1 On Christmas day.
2 Yes, he is.
3 Yes, he does.
4 I like Santa.

5
A Whose bag is this?

B _____

1 It's mine.
2 It is green.
3 All right.
4 His bag is green.

6
A Can a hippo fly?

B _____

1 It is big.
2 Yes, it is.
3 No, it can't.
4 He is my pet.

7
A Nice to meet you.

B _____

1 Nice to meet you, too.
2 See you later.
3 Good night.
4 Yes, please.

8
A What time do you go to bed?

B _____

1 Good night.
2 Good morning.
3 At ten thirty.
4 In December.

1 Write the Japanese in the (   ) and draw lines.

Where (   ) •   • By airplane.

How (   ) •   • To Hawaii.

How long (   ) •   • For five days.

2 Write the correct answers.

① (   ) Monday
月曜日に

② (   ) the morning
朝に

③ (   ) July
7月に

④ (   ) car
車で

⑤ (   ) night
夜に

⑥ (   ) one week
1週間

⑦ (   ) one year
1年間

⑧ (   ) March sixth
3月6日に

by   on   in   at   for

3 Words

① on Tuesday
(   ) _____

② in August
(   ) _____

③ for one week
(   ) _____

④ for three days
(   ) _____

⑤ for one month
(   ) _____

⑥ for one year
(   ) _____

⑦ stay
(   ) _____

⑧ lucky
(   ) _____

2nd Learning World ❸ WORKBOOK — ANSWERS

Unit 1- ❶ p.4

1 （解答例 絵ともに省略）

have, want, like を使って自分のことを書いて、その絵も描きましょう。

2 **Words**
❶ 月　❷ 空
❸ 山　❹ 丘
❺ 花　❻ 湖
❼ 雲　❽ 星

Unit 1- ❷ p.5

1 （すべて解答例）
❶ My name is Maki.
❷ My family name is Tanaka.
❸ I'm ten years old.
❹ I live in Osaka.
❺ It's April nineteenth.
❻ It's Monday.
❼ It's May ninth.

2 **Words**
❶ 3番めの　❷ 2番めの
❸ 名字　❹ 小学校
❺ 学年　❻ 快晴の
❼ 4月　❽ 1月

Unit 1- ❸ p.6

1
❶ I don't know.
❷ I don't understand.
❸ More slowly, please.
❹ How do you spell 'cat'?
❺ I'm finished.
❻ How do you say gakunen in English?（解答例）

2 **Words**
❶ 消防士　❷ タクシー運転手
❸ 生徒　❹ 家族
❺ 紹介する　❻ 理解する
❼ 言う　❽ ゆっくりと

p.7 Let's try: ❶
① ❸ am
② ❶ in
③ ❹ is
④ ❷ What
⑤ ❷ are
⑥ ❷ are
⑦ ❸ am
⑧ ❸ don't
⑨ ❹ I
⑩ ❶ do

Unit 2- ❶ p.8

1
❶ He isn't a dentist.
❷ Is he a teacher? Yes, he is.
❸ She isn't a doctor.
❹ What is she? She is a teacher.
❺ She is a scientist.
❻ What is she? She is a scientist.

2 **Words**
❶ 警察官　❷ 技師
❸ 大工　❹ 農場経営者
❺ 漁師　❻ 看護師
❼ ゆうかんな　❽ 強い

Unit 2- ❷ p.9

1
① What is she doing? She is reading.
③ What is she doing? She is cooking.
⑤ What is he doing? He is sleeping.
② What is she doing? She is crying.
④ What is he doing? He is running.
⑥ What is he doing? He is cleaning.

2 **Words**
❶ 掃除している　❷ 泣いている
❸ 練習している　❹ 運転している
❺ ～を聞いている　❻ ～と話している
❼ ～を待っている　❽ いそがしい

Unit 2- ❸ p.10

1
❶ Hands Off
❷ Staff Only
❸ Keep Off the Grass
❹ Do Not Cross
❺ Dead End
❻ One Way
❼ Pull
❽ Fire Exit
❾ Out Of Order
❿ Closed
⓫ Keep Left
⓬ Wait Here

2 **Words**
❶ ふとんを整える　❷ もっとゆっくり食べる
❸ 寝る　❹ 出かける
❺ 飛びはねる　❻ 音を立てる
❼ 夜ふかしをする　❽ どなる

p.11 Let's try: ❷
① ❸ Where
② ❹ When
③ ❶ What
④ ❹ listening
⑤ ❷ cooking
⑥ ❶ time
⑦ ❷ on
⑧ ❹ See
⑨ ❸ Whose
⑩ ❷ May

Unit 3- ❶ p.12

1
❶ a dog / dogs
❷ a pig / pigs
❸ a cat / cats
❹ a goose / geese
❺ a sheep / sheep（無変化）
❻ a mouse / mice（無変化）

2 （絵は省略）
① three
② sixteen
③ fifteen
④ ten

Unit 3- ❷ p.13

1
❶ a woman / women
❷ a man / men
❸ a child / children

2
❶ seven
❷ twenty four
❸ sixty
❹ five（解答例）
❺ three（解答例）

3 **Words**
❶ 農場　❷ 家畜小屋
❸ 七面鳥　❹ ひよこ
❺ ～の上に　❻ ～の中に
❼ ～の前に　❽ ～の間に

Unit 3- ❸ p.14

1
❶ The cow is.
❷ The horse is.
❸ The rooster is.
❹ The snake is.
❺ The dog is.
❻ The tiger is.
❼ The wild boar is.

十二支の並びになっています。

2 **Words**
❶ あなたのもの　❷ 私のもの
❸ どちらのもの（どれ）　❹ 駐車場
❺ あのもの（あれ）　❻ いのしし
❼ にわとり(おんどり)　❽ たつ

③、❺：名詞のくり返しを避けて使う one です。

p.15 Let's try: ❸
① ❸ many
② ❶ much
③ ❷ Is
④ ❷ Let's
⑤ ❶ go
⑥ ❷ washing
⑦ ❷ twelve
⑧ ❶ I
⑨ ❸ time
⑩ ❷ after

Unit 4- ❶ p.16

1 （すべて解答例）
❶ Ⓒ No, I can't.
❷ Ⓕ Yes, I can.
❸ Ⓔ No, I can't.
❹ Ⓓ Yes, I can.
❺ Ⓑ No, I can't.
❻ Ⓐ Yes, I can.

2
Ⓐ 一輪車にのる　Ⓓ サッカーでゴールを決める
Ⓑ ケーキを焼く　Ⓔ バスケットボールでシュートを決める
Ⓒ 水にもぐる　Ⓕ バスケットボールをする

3
❶ A penguin can't fly in the sky.
❷ A snake can swim in the water.
❸ A panda can climb a tree.
❹ A rooster can't lay eggs.

Unit 4- ❷ p.17

1
❶ This is my wheelchair.
❷ I am proud of my family.
❸ He can play soccer, too.
❹ He is a great athlete.
❺ Can you read Braille?
❻ I can go everywhere with him.

2 **Words**
❶ ～を誇りに思う　❷ 車いす
❸ 偉大な　❹ 運動選手
❺ 盲導犬　❻ どこでも
❼ かしこい　❽ 点字

Unit 4- ❸ p.18

1 （解答例）
❶ Akiko can speak English very well.
❷
❸ （以下省略）
❹
❺
❻

2 **Words**
❶ 話す　❷ 上手に
❸ とても上手に　❹ 少し
❺ まったく～ない　❻ もちろん
❼ リコーダー　❽ 書く

p.19 Let's try: ❹
① ❹ twelfth
② ❶ reading
③ ❷ by
④ ❷ to
⑤ ❸ one
⑥ ❷ to
⑦ ❸ We
⑧ ❸ from
⑨ ❶ for
⑩ ❹ to

Unit 5- ① p.20

1
① 持つ　has
② あそぶ　plays
③ 住む　lives
④ 好き　likes
⑤ 洗う　washes
⑥ 話す　speaks
⑦ 行く　goes
⑧ ～をする　does
⑨ 書く　writes
⑩ 起きる　gets up
⑪ 食べる　eats
⑫ ほしい　wants

2
① My brother **has** two sisters.
② My brother **lives** in Denver, too.
③ My brother **plays** tennis, too.
④ My brother **wants** a new racket, too.
⑤ My brother **gets** up at seven o'clock, too.
⑥ My brother **goes** to school by bike, too.

Unit 5- ② p.21

1
① Do you like milk? Yes, I **do**.
② I **do** not like coffee.
③ My sister **does** not like milk.
④ **Does** your mother play tennis? No, she **does** not.
⑤ When **do** you play tennis?
⑥ Where **do** you and your sister live?

2
This is a kangaroo.
（すべて解答例）
It lives in Australia.
It can jump.
It has a strong tail.
It has a baby in its pocke

Unit 5- ③ p.22

1（すべて解答例）In my family, my mother cleans my room.
My father cooks breakfast. My big sister washes the dishes.
My mother buys groceries, and my mother cleans the bathroom.

2（解答例）
① Mr. Tanaka does.
（以下省略）

3 Words
① いつも
② ときどき
③ 決して～しない
④ (あなたの)部屋を掃除する
⑤ 皿を洗う
⑥ ペットにえさをやる
⑦ 食品を買う
⑧ 浴室を掃除する

p.23 Let's try 5

① ❸ Thank you.
② ❶ Yes, let's.
③ ❷ This is Tom speaking.
④ ❶ To school.
⑤ ❸ Yes, I do.
⑥ ❶ Sunny and hot.
⑦ ❷ I am in the kitchen.

Unit 6- ① p.24

1
① Do you have to do your homework?
Yes, I do. I have to do my homework.
② Do you have to cook dinner?
Yes, I do. I have to cook dinner.
③ Do you have to go to *juku*?
No, I don't. I don't have to go to *juku*.
④ Does your teacher have to do her homework?
No, she doesn't. She doesn't have to do her homework.
⑤ Does your teacher have to cook dinner?
Yes, she does. She has to cook dinner.
⑥ Does your teacher have to go to *juku*?
Yes, she does. She has to go to *juku*.

2 Words
① ～しなければならない
② すぐに
③ 話すのをやめる
④ 笑うのをやめる
⑤ 走るのをやめる
⑥ 書くのをやめる
⑦ 見るのをやめる
⑧ あそぶのをやめる

Unit 6- ② p.25

◯
① handsome
② dirty
③ noisy
④ tired
⑤ cheerful
⑥ timid
⑦ honest
⑧ beautiful
⑨ messy
⑩ scary
⑪ pretty
⑫ cool
⑬ brave
⑭ rich
⑮ old
⑯ young
⑰ rude
⑱ kind
⑲ sleepy
⑳ great

Unit 6- ③ p.26

1（①②③はすべて解答例）
① The Matterhorn is higher than Mt. Fuji.
② Mt. McKinley is higher than Mt. Fuji.
③ Mt. McKinley is higher than the Matterhorn.
④ Mt. Everest is the highest.

2 Words
① より(背の)高い
② より強い
③ より短い、より背の低い
④ より長い
⑤ より大きい
⑥ より小さい
⑦ より良い
⑧ より悪い

p.27 Let's try 6

① ❷ It is one hundred years old.
② ❷ And you?
③ ❸ Here you are.
④ ❸ Yes, he does.
⑤ ❶ It's mine.
⑥ ❸ No, it can't.
⑦ ❶ Nice to meet you, too
⑧ ❸ At ten thirty.

Unit 7- ① p.28

1
Where（ どこ ）— By airplane.
How（ どのように ）— To Hawaii.
How long（ どのくらい ）— For five days.

2
① on Monday
② in the morning
③ in July
④ by car
⑤ at night
⑥ for one week
⑦ for one year
⑧ on March sixth

3 Words
① 火曜日に
② 8月に
③ 1週間
④ 3日間
⑤ 1か月間
⑥ 1年間
⑦ 滞在する
⑧ 幸運な

Unit 7- ② p.29

1（すべて解答例）
① I will get up at seven.
② I will go to school at seven forty.
③ I will come home at four.
④ I will have supper at six thirty.
⑤ I will go to bed at ten.

2 Words
① 今日
② 明日
③ あさって
④ 来週
⑤ 来週の日曜日
⑥ 来月
⑦ 2040年
⑧ より若い

Unit 7- ③ p.30

1
① I want to go to France. I want to eat French food. I want to speak French.
② I want to go to Japan. I want to eat Japanese food. I want to speak Japanese.
③ I want to go to Italy. I want to eat Italian food. I want to speak Italian.
④ I want to go to Spain. I want to eat Spanish food. I want to speak Spanish.

2 Words
① ほしい
② 行きたい
③ 話したい
④ 食べたい
⑤ 先生を手伝う
⑥ お母さんを手伝う
⑦ 昼寝をする
⑧ 家に帰る

p.31 Let's try 7

| どこ？ Where | なに？ What | いつ？ When |
| だれ？ Who | どのように？ How | なぜ？ Why |

① ❷ Where
② ❶ When
③ ❹ How
④ ❷ What time
⑤ ❶ How long
⑥ ❸ Have

Unit 8- ① p.32

1
① something to eat
② something to read
③ something to drink
④ something to read
⑤ something to eat
⑥ something to wear
⑦ something to wear
⑧ something to drink
⑨ something to play
⑩ something to wear
めがねやコンタクトレンズも wearを使います。

2 Words
① 何か食べるもの
② 何か飲むもの
③ 何か着るもの
④ 何か読むもの
⑤ カップ1杯の紅茶
⑥ グラス1杯の水
⑦ 1足のくつ下
⑧ めがね1個

Unit 8- ② p.33

1（すべて解答例）
① I go to the library to read some books.
② I go to the park to take a walk.
③ I go to the station to catch a train.
④ I go to the florist to buy some flowers.

2 Words
① パン屋
② レストラン
③ 銀行
④ 市役所
⑤ デパート
⑥ 郵便局
⑦ 図書館
⑧ 病院

Unit 8- ③ p.34

1
① It is cloudy now.
It was sunny this morning.
② We were caterpillars.
We are butterflies now.

2
① He was playing tennis at four o'clock.
② She was studying at eight o'clock.
③ He was taking a nap at one o'clock.

3 Words
① ～です
② ～でした
③ 変な、奇妙な
④ 夢
⑤ ジャングル
⑥ 色とりどりの
⑦ オオハシ(鳥)
⑧ ～を越えて

p.35 Let's try 8

① ❸ glad
② ❶ take a nap
③ ❹ in
④ ❶ a glass of
⑤ ❸ goes
⑥ ❷ the post office
⑦ ❹ to eat
⑧ ❶ Can you help me?

Unit 9- ① p.36

1
① She went to the hospital yesterday.
② He made a sandwich yesterday.
③ He read a newspaper yesterday.

2（すべて解答例）
I did my homework.
I went shopping with my friend.
I watched TV.

3
① 宿題をする did your homework
② クッキーを取る took a cookie
③ サンドイッチを作る made a sandwich
④ 買い物に行く went shopping
⑤ ホットドッグを食べる had a hot dog
⑥ 本を読む read [red] a book

Unit 9- ② p.37

1（すべて解答例）
① Yes, I did. I made my bed ～.
② Yes, I did. I ate my lunch ～.
③ No, I didn't. I didn't clean my room～.
④ No, I didn't. I didn't take a bath ～.
⑤ Yes, I did. I studied English ～.

2
① 自分のふとんを整える made my bed
② 昼食を食べる ate my lunch
③ 自分の部屋を掃除する cleaned my roor
④ 風呂に入る took a bath
⑤ 英語を勉強する studied Englis
⑥ サッカーをする played soccer

①
① Sakura is bigger than Chibi. (解答例)
② Chibi Is smaller than Sakura. (解答例)
③ Zippy is bigger than Sakura. (解答例)
④ Zippy is the biggest.
⑤ Chibi is the smallest.

② words
① きこり ② (木の)枝 ③ 森 ④ 斧(おの) ⑤ 妖精(ようせい) ⑥ 正直な ⑦ 重要な
⑧ 現れた ⑨ 落ちた ⑩ 戻った ⑪ 質問した、たずねた ⑫ なくした ⑬ 与える ⑭ 言った

① ③ Who
② ④ was, ④ was
③ ② did
④ ③ Look
⑤ ④ did
⑥ ① is
⑦ ① to
⑧ ② write with

Unit 10-① p.40

①
① Her name is Tina.
② She is eleven years old.
③ She is in the fifth grade.
④ Her school is Lakeside Elementary School.
⑤ She lives in Denver, Colorado, in the U.S.
⑥ Yes, she does.
⑦ It is a dog.
⑧ Its name is Zippy.
⑨ She likes to play tennis after school.
⑩ Yes, she can.
⑪ They are math and music.
⑫ She doesn't like social studies.

Unit 10-② p.41

①
① She is my grandmother.
② Her name is Jerri.
③ She is seventy years old.
④ She lives in the country.
⑤ She likes music.
⑥ She listens to music every day.

② words
① 両親 ② 祖父母 ③ おじ ④ おば
⑤ 1人の子ども ⑥ 子どもたち ⑦ むすこ ⑧ むすめ

10-③ p.42

① (解答例)

むかしむかし、お母さんネズミが赤ちゃんネズミと小さな町に住んでいました。
お母さんネズミは毎日赤ちゃんネズミにレッスンをしていました。
「ワンワン ワンワン ほら、後について!」
赤ちゃんネズミは「ワンワン ワンワン」。
「もっと大きな声で」お母さんネズミは言いました。
「ワンワン ワンワン」「もっと大きく!」
「ワンワン ワンワン!」赤ちゃんネズミはとても一生懸命練習をしました。
来る日も来る日もお母さんと赤ちゃんネズミは練習しました。

ある日、お母さんネズミと赤ちゃんが街を散歩していた時、大きなネコがあらわれました。
ネコは赤ちゃんネズミをつかまえて食べようとしました。
赤ちゃんネズミはとても怖くなって動けなくなりました。
でもお母さんネズミはネコをにらみつけて大きな声でさけびました。
「ワンワン ワンワン」。
赤ちゃんネズミもお母さんに続いて「ワンワン ワンワン」と大きな声で言いました。
ネコはびっくりして逃げていきました。犬だと思ったからです。
お母さんネズミは赤ちゃんネズミの方をふり返って言いました。
「ね、なぜ外国語を勉強するのが大切かがわかったでしょ!」

① I want something to drink.
② I go to the station to meet my friends.
③ I can speak English a little.
④ Did you watch TV last night?
⑤ I am in the fifth grade of Fuji Elementary School.
⑥ My little brother will be eight years old next month.
⑦ Where do you want to go?
⑧ Which bag is yours?

p.45 — Listening Homework ①

CD1 英語をよく聞いて、それに合う絵の番号を選びましょう。

No.1 What are they doing? They are cooking. ④
No.2 Where is the dog? Look! It's running in the park. ①
No.3 What day is it today? It's Sunday. ④
No.4 I like my new soccer ball. Let's play soccer. ④

CD2 4つの英文の中から、絵の内容を最もよく表している文の番号を選びましょう。

No.5
1. This is a train station.　(2.) This is a school.
3. This is a department store.　4. This is a supermarket.

No.6
1. Mr. Brown is twenty-one years old.　2. Mr. Brown is twenty-eight years old.
3. Mr. Brown is twelve years old.　(4.) Mr. Brown is twenty years old.

No.7
1. Mary can't skate.　2. Mary can swim very well.
3. Mary can't swim.　(4.) Mary can skate very well.

No.8
1. I have two birds in the cage.　2. I have three birds in the cage.
(3.) I have two rabbits in the cage.　4. I have three birds in the box.

p.46 — Listening Homework ②

CD3 英語をよく聞いて、それに合う絵の番号を選びましょう。

No.1 What does your father do? He is a fire fighter. ②
No.2 What time do you get up in the morning? At five thirty. ①
No.3 What is your father doing? He is reading the newspaper. ①
No.4 How do you go to school? I go to school by bicycle. ③

CD4 4つの英文の中から、絵の内容を最もよく表している文の番号を選びましょう。

No.5
1. There are three shirts.　2. There is a shirt.
3. There are five shirts.　(4.) There are two shirts.

No.6
1. It is snowy today.　(2.) It is rainy today.
3. It is windy today.　4. It is sunny today.

No.7
1. My father is a scientist.　(2.) My father is a singer.
3. My father is a dentist.　4. My mother is a singer.

No.8
1. My birthday is July 10th.　2. My birthday is October 10th.
(3.) My birthday is March 20th.　4. My birthday is March 12th.

p.47 — Listening Homework ③

CD5 次の絵について質問します。その答えとして最も適切なものの番号を選びましょう。

No.1 What is the dog doing? ②
No.2 How is the weather? ②
No.3 How many people are skiing? ③
No.4 What is the man under the tree doing? ①

CD6 4つの英文の中から、絵の内容を最もよく表している文の番号を選びましょう。

No.5
1. My sister can't ride a bicycle.　2. My sister can ride a bicycle.
3. My sister can play the piano.　(4.) My sister can ride a unicycle.

No.6
1. Today is March eleventh.　(2.) Today is May twelfth.
3. Today is September nineteenth.　4. Today is May twentieth.

No.7
1. My sister likes climbing trees.　2. My sister likes playing the piano.
3. My sister likes listening to music.　(4.) My sister likes swimming.

No.8
1. A boy with a cap is crying.　2. A boy with a cap is smiling.
(3.) A girl with a cap is crying.　4. A girl with a cap is smiling.

p.48 — Listening Homework ④

CD7 英語をよく聞いて、それに合う絵の番号を選びましょう。

No.1 It is summer now. I like summer best. ③
No.2 My brother Tadashi is playing the guitar. ①
No.3 My mother is angry. ④
No.4 Where is my cap? It is under the sofa. ③

CD8 4つの英文の中から、絵の内容を最もよく表している文の番号を選びましょう。

No.5
1. It is Tuesday.　2. It is Sunday.
3. It is Monday.　(4.) It is Thursday.

No.6
1. This is a pumpkin.　2. This is a cucumber.
(3.) These are pumpkins.　4. These are tomatoes.

No.7
(1.) What a beautiful flower!　2. What a big flower!
3. What a little flower!　4. What a beautiful girl!

No.8
1. I am going to Sapporo by car.　2. I am going to Sapporo by airplane.
3. I am going to Sapporo by ferry.　(4.) I am going to Sapporo by train.

p.49 — Listening Homework ⑤

CD9 次の絵について質問します。その答えとして最も適切なものの番号を選びましょう。

No.1 How many people are sitting? ④
No.2 How is the weather? ③
No.3 What is the old man on the right doing? ②
No.4 Where is it? ④

CD10 対話と質問を聞き、その答えとして最も適切なものの番号を選びましょう。

No.5
A: Where do you live, Jane?
B: I live in Kanagawa.
(Q: Where does Jane live?) ②

No.6
A: Where are you going, Yuka?
B: I am going to the supermarket with my mother.
(Q: Where is Yuka going?) ①

No.7
A: Do you have any brothers or sisters, Kenji?
B: Yes, I have two big brothers. But I don't have any sisters.
(Q: Does Kenji have any brothers?) ①

No.8
A: What are you doing, Jenny?
B: I am doing my homework.
(Q: What is Jenny doing?) ③

Listening Homework ⑥

CD11　4つの英文の中から、絵の内容を最もよく表している文の番号を選びましょう。

No.1
1. This is my computer.　　2. This is my clock.
3. This is my camera.　　④ This is my TV.

No.2
1. I will take a bath.　　2. I will take a walk.
③ I will iron the clothes.　　4. I will do the dishes.

No.3
1. Open the window, please.　　2. Open the door, please.
3. Go to the door, please.　　④ Close the window, please.

No.4
1. I am 153cm tall.　　② I am 143cm tall.
3. I am 155cm tall.　　4. I am 134cm tall.

CD12　対話と質問を聞き、その答えとして最も適切なものの番号を選びましょう。

No.5
A: Can you speak Chinese, Akiko?
B: No, I can't. But I can speak English.
（Q: Can Akiko speak Chinese?）①

No.6
A: Does your sister play tennis, Terry?
B: No, she doesn't. But she plays baseball.
（Q: What sport does Terry's sister play?）②

No.7
A: Where are you, Sara?
B: I am here in the living room. I am watching TV with my mother.
（Q: Where is Sara's mother?）①

No.8
A: David, what's your favorite food?
B: I like hamburgers.
（Q: Does David like hamburgers?）④

Listening Homework ⑦

CD13　次の絵について質問します。その答えとして最も適切なものの番号を選びましょう。

No.1 Where is the dog?　②

No.2 What is Father doing?　③

No.3 What is Grandmother doing?　①

No.4 Is the cat sleeping?　③

CD14　対話と質問を聞き、その答えとして最も適切なものの番号を選びましょう。

No.5
A: Do you like math, Ken?
B: No, I don't. But I like P.E.
（Q: What school subject does Ken like?）③

No.6
A: Let's play baseball after school, John.
B: Well, I have to go to the dentist after school.
（Q: What does John have to do after school?）②

No.7
A: When is your birthday, Kenji?
B: My birthday is January 29th, the day before my mother's birthday.
（Q: When is Kenji's mother's birthday?）③

No.8
A: Where did you go last Sunday, Jerry?
B: I went to Victoria. I took the ferry.
（Q: Where did Jerry go last Sunday?）③

Listening Homework ⑧

CD15　英語をよく聞いて、それに合う絵の番号を選びましょう。

No.1 A girl with long hair has a dog in her arms.　③

No.2 A man on a boat is catching a big fish.　①

No.3 I am cold. I want something hot to drink.　④

No.4 I have to go to bed at nine o'clock.　①

CD16　4つの英文の中から、絵の内容を最もよく表している文の番号を選びましょう。

No.5
1. The monster has big eyes.　　② The monster has a big mouth.
3. The monster has big ears.　　4. The monster has pretty eyes.

No.6
1. I want to buy three hot dogs.　　2. I want to buy two hot dogs.
③ I want to buy three dogs.　　4. I want to buy three pizzas.

No.7
① I like swimming in the lake.　　2. I like swimming in the pool.
3. I like water skiing on the lake.　　4. I like ice skating on the lake.

No.8
1. My office is on the second floor.　　2. My office is on the fifth floor.
③ My office is on the fourth floor.　　4. My office is on the first floor.

Listening Homework ⑨

CD17　イラストを参考にしながら、その答えとして最も適切なものの番号を選びましょう。

No.1 What does your father do?　②

No.2 Where is my book?　①

No.3 I have a lot of homework today.　①

No.4 Hello. Can I speak to Mary, please?　③

CD18　対話と質問を聞き、その答えとして最も適切なものの番号を選びましょう。

No.5
Boy: When do you have English lessons, Ann?
Girl: Every Wednesday.
（Q: When does Ann have English lessons?）③

No.6
B: I am hungry. I want something to eat.
G: Me, too.
（Q: What does the boy want?）④

No.7
B: Can Mr. Brown speak English well?
G: Of course. He is from England.
（Q: Can Mr. Brown speak English well?）①

No.8
B: I have to go to school at seven o'clock tomorrow morning.
G: Then you have to get up at six.
（Q: What time will the boy get up tomorrow morning?）③

Listening Homework ⑩

CD19　イラストを参考にしながら、英語の質問に対して最も適切なものの番号を選びましょう。

No.1 Where does your uncle live?　②

No.2 Where are you going?　③

No.3 Can your mother speak English?　②

No.4 Who is taller, you or your brother?　②

CD20　4つの英文の中から、絵の内容を最もよく表している文の番号を選びましょう。

No.5
① A monkey is reading a book.　2. A monkey is eating a banana.
3. A monkey is writing a book.　4. A monkey is reading a newspaper.

No.6
1. It was rainy yesterday.　　2. It was sunny yesterday.
③ It was snowy yesterday.　　4. It was cloudy yesterday.

No.7
1. There are five pencils in the box.　② There are five pencils on the desk.
3. There are four pencils on the desk.　4. There are five pencils under the des

No.8
1. He is a scientist.　　2. He is a fire fighter.
3. He is an engineer.　　④ He is a farmer.

LET'S READ. ①　**p.55**　㉑でストーリーの音声を聴くことができます。

① There are many stars and planets in space.

② It is called a space station.

③ Yes, it does.

④ Yes, we can.

⑤ We have to wear special clothes and an oxygen tank.

⑥ Because there is no air in space.

⑦ Yes, we are.

⑧ No, I don't. (I like the earth.)　　（解答例）

LET'S READ. ②　**p.56**　㉒でストーリーの音声を聴くことができます。

① An ostrich is a big bird.

② It is very tall.

③ It is sometimes nine feet tall.

④ Yes, they are.

⑤ Yes, it is.

⑥ No, it can't.

⑦ Because it is too big to fly.

⑧ They have four toes.

⑨ It has only two toes.

⑩ It can live to be seventy years old.

⑪ Yes, they are.

⑫ They live in Africa.

LET'S READ ①
● space station：宇宙ステーション
● oxygen tank：酸素タンク
● air：大気

LET'S READ ②
● ostrich：だちょう
● nine feet tall：センチに換算すると約274cm（1フィート：約30cm）
● float：浮く

1 Write your own answers. What will you do tomorrow?

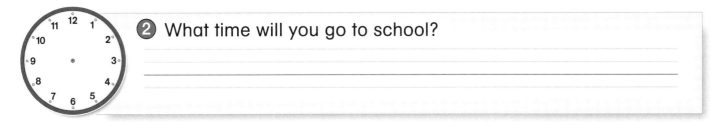

1 What time will you get up tomorrow morning?

_____

_____

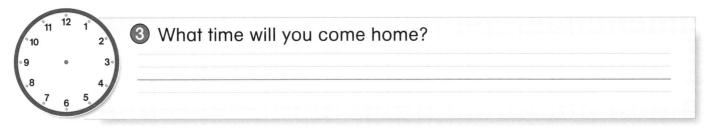

2 What time will you go to school?

_____

_____

3 What time will you come home?

_____

_____

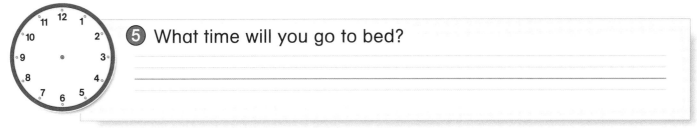

4 What time will you have supper?

_____

_____

5 What time will you go to bed?

_____

_____

2 Words ....

1 today
( ) _____

2 tomorrow
( ) _____

3 the day after tomorrow
( ) _____

4 next week
( ) _____

5 next Sunday
( ) _____

6 next month
( ) _____

7 the year 2040
( ) _____

8 younger
( ) _____

1 **Fill in the blanks.**

1 France

I want to go to _France._

I want to eat _French_ food.

I want to speak _French._

2 Japan

I want to go to _____

I want to eat _____ food.

I want to speak _____

3 Italy

I want to go to _____

I want to eat _____ food.

I want to speak _____

4 Spain

I want to go to _____

I want to eat _____ food.

I want to speak _____

2 **Words**

❶ want
( ) _____

❷ want to go
( ) _____

❸ want to speak
( ) _____

❹ want to eat
( ) _____

❺ help my teacher
( ) _____

❻ help my mother
( ) _____

❼ take a nap
( ) _____

❽ go home
( ) _____

どこ？ _____	なに？ _____	いつ？ _____
だれ？ _____	どのように？ _____	なぜ？ _____

What
Where
When
Who
Why
How

Choose and write the correct answers.

1

A _____ are you going?

B I'm going to the market.

❶ When　　　❷ Where　　　❸ What　　　❹ How

2

A _____ is your birthday?

B My birthday is July third.

❶ When　　　❷ Where　　　❸ What　　　❹ How

3

A _____ are you going to Hawaii?

B By plane.

❶ When　　　❷ Where　　　❸ What　　　❹ How

4

A _____ do you get up in the morning?

B At seven thirty.

❶ How long　　　❷ What time　　　❸ What day　　　❹ How many

5

A _____ are you going to stay in Japan?

B For one year.

❶ How long　　　❷ What time　　　❸ How many　　　❹ How much

6

A _____ a good time!

B You, too.

❶ Make　　　❷ Want　　　❸ Have　　　❹ Play

1 Write the correct verbs.

1. an apple — *something to eat*

2. a book

3. coffee

4. a newspaper

5. a hamburger

6. shoes

7. glasses

8. juice

9. a piano

10. contact lenses

2 Words

1 something to eat
(   )

2 something to drink
(   )

3 something to wear
(   )

4 something to read
(   )

5 a cup of tea
(   )

6 a glass of water
(   )

7 a pair of socks
(   )

8 a pair of glasses
(   )

1 Complete the sentences.

1 Why do you go to the library?

I go to the library

2 Why do you go to the park?

I go to the park

3 Why do you go to the station?

I go

4 Why do you go to the florist?

I

to take a walk   to catch a train   to buy some flowers   to read some books

2 words ....

1 bakery ( ) _____

2 restaurant ( ) _____

3 bank ( ) _____

4 city hall ( ) _____

5 department store ( ) _____

6 post office ( ) _____

7 library ( ) _____

8 hospital ( ) _____

am / is / are / was / were

1 **Fill in the blanks.**

① It _____ cloudy now.

It _____ sunny this morning.

② We _____ caterpillars.

We _____ butterflies now.

2 **Look at the pictures and answer the questions.**

① What was he doing at four o'clock?

He was _____

play tennis

② What was she doing at eight o'clock?

_____
_____

study

③ What was he doing at one o'clock?

_____
_____
_____

take a nap

3 **Words**

① is, am, are _____
(   ) _____

② was, were _____
(   ) _____

③ strange _____
(   ) _____

④ dream _____
(   ) _____

⑤ jungle _____
(   ) _____

⑥ colorful _____
(   ) _____

⑦ toucan _____
(   ) _____

⑧ over _____
(   ) _____

Let's try - 3

Choose and write the correct answers.

1 Hello. My name is Takashi. I am _____ to meet you.

❶pretty ❷big ❸glad ❹busy

2 I am sleepy. I want to _____.

❶take a nap ❷play baseball ❸watch TV ❹buy a present

3 **A** Where do you live?

B I live _____ Tokyo.

❶for ❷to ❸on ❹in

4 I am thirsty. May I have _____ water, please?

❶a glass of ❷a pair of ❸drink ❹like

5 **A** How does your sister go to school?

B She _____ to school by train.

❶plays ❷go ❸goes ❹play

6 **A** I want to mail a letter. I have to buy a stamp.

B Let's go to _____ near the station.

❶on foot ❷the post office ❸the restaurant ❹pencils

7 **A** I am hungry.

B Let's have something _____.

❶to wear ❷to drink ❸to read ❹to eat

8 **A** I can't open the door. _____

B Sure.

❶Can you help me? ❷Can you run? ❸That sounds great. ❹Have a good time.

1 Look at the pictures and answer the questions.

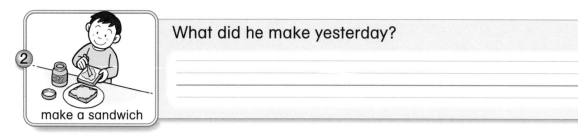

go to the hospital

Where did she go yesterday?

make a sandwich

What did he make yesterday?

read a newspaper

What did he read yesterday?

2 What did you do yesterday? Write three things you did yesterday.

3 Write the Japanese in the (   ). Then write the English past form.

❶ do your homework
(   )

❷ take a cookie
(   )

❸ make a sandwich
(   )

❹ go shopping
(   )

❺ have a hot dog
(   )

❻ read a book
(   )

2

1 Write your own answers.

1 Did you make your bed this morning?

2 Did you eat your lunch yesterday?

3 Did you clean your room yesterday?

4 Did you take a bath last night?

5 Did you study English yesterday?

2 Write the Japanese in the (   ). Then write the English past form.

1 make my bed
(   )

2 eat my lunch
(   )

3 clean my room
(   )

4 take a bath
(   )

5 study English
(   )

6 play soccer
(   )

1 **Look at the pictures and write the answers.**

Sakura

Chibi

Zippy

1 Sakura _____ is bigger than _____

2 _____ is smaller than _____

3 _____ is _____ than _____

4 _____ is the biggest.   **5** _____ is the smallest.

2 words ....

1 woodcutter ( )		**2** branch ( )	
3 forest ( )		**4** ax ( )	
5 the spirit ( )		**6** honest ( )	
7 important ( )		**8** appeared ( )	
9 fell ( )		**10** came back ( )	
11 asked ( )		**12** lost ( )	
13 give ( )		**14** said ( )	

Choose and write the correct answers.

1

A _____ cooks breakfast?

B My father does.

❶ Where   ❷ Why   ❸ Who   ❹ Does

2

A Where were you yesterday?

B I _____ at the library. I _____ reading a book.

❶ am   ❷ were   ❸ like   ❹ was

3

A Did you have a good time?

B Yes, I _____. It was a great movie.

❶ am   ❷ did   ❸ was   ❹ saw

4

A _____ at the flowers. They are very beautiful.

B Yes, they are. I like the yellow one.

❶ Have   ❷ Like   ❸ Look   ❹ Speak

5

A Did you eat your lunch?

B Yes, I _____. I ate sandwiches.

❶ can   ❷ eat   ❸ sandwiches   ❹ did

6

A What does your mother do?

B She _____ a teacher.

❶ is   ❷ likes   ❸ English   ❹ does

7

I want _____ be a doctor.

❶ to   ❷ don't   ❸ have   ❹ can

8

I want something to _____. May I use your pencil?

❶ read   ❷ write with   ❸ play   ❹ wear

Read the letter on p.58 in the textbook and answer the questions.

1 What's her name?

2 How old is she?

3 What grade is she in?

4 What is the name of her school?

5 Where does she live?

6 Does she have a pet?

7 If so, what is it?

8 What is her pet's name?

9 What does she like to do after school?

10 Can she play the piano?

11 What are her favorite school subjects?

12 What doesn't she like?

1 Answer the questions.

This is my grandmother. Her name is Jerri.
She is seventy years old. She lives in the country.
She likes music. She listens to music every day.

① Who is the lady in the picture?

She is

② What is her name?

③ How old is she?

④ Where does she live?

⑤ What does she like?

⑥ What does she do every day?

2 words

❶ parents	❷ grandparents
( )	( )
❸ uncle	❹ aunt
( )	( )
❺ a child	❻ children
( )	( )
❼ son	❽ daughter
( )	( )

Read the story on p.62 in the textbook and write about it in Japanese.

Story: It is important to learn a foreign language.

Repeat after me!

Bow-wow!

Let's try. 10

Put the words in the correct order and complete the sentences.

1 私は何か飲むものがほしいです。

_____

| drink | I | something | want | to |

2 私はともだちを迎えに駅に行きます。

_____

| the station | my friends | meet | go | to | to | I |

3 私は英語を少し話すことができます。

_____

| I | speak | a little | English | can |

4 昨夜テレビを見ましたか。

_____

| you | TV | last night | watch | did | ? |

5 私は富士小学校の5年生です。

_____

| I | in | Fuji | of | the fifth grade | Elementary School | am |

6 私の弟は来月8歳になります。

_____

| eight | years old | little brother | will be | my | next month |

7 あなたはどこに行きたいですか。

_____

| you | want | go | where | to | do | ? |

8 どのかばんがあなたのものですか。

_____

| bag | is | yours | which | ? |

the story of
Unit 9-3
textbook p.56

A	again	再び	
	answer	答える	(過去形 answered)
	appear	現れる	(過去形 appeared)
	ask	たずねる	(過去形 asked)
	ax	斧（おの）	
B	branch	（木の）枝	
C	come back	帰ってくる	(過去形 came back)
	cry	泣く	(過去形 cried)
	cut … off ~	～ から … を切り落とす	
F	fall	落ちる	(過去形 fell)
	forest	森	
G	give	与える	(過去形 gave)
	golden	金色の	
H	honest	正直な	
I	important	重要な、大切な	
	into …	…の中へ	
	iron	鉄の	
L	lose	失う、なくす	(過去形 lost)
M	mine	私のもの	
O	old	古い	(比較級 older)
	once upon a time	むかしむかし	
S	say	言う	(過去形 said)
	silver	銀の	
	(the) spirit	妖精（ようせい）、聖霊（せいれい）	
W	water	水	
	woodcutter	きこり	

the story of
Unit 10-3
textbook p.62

A	appear	現れる	(過去形 appeared)
B	bowwow	ワンワン（犬の鳴き声）	
C	catch	捕まえる	(過去形 caught)
	could not …	…できなかった	
D	day	日 *day after day :* くる日もくる日も	
E	even	…さえも	
F	follow	ついてゆく	(過去形 followed)
	foreign language	外国語	
G	give	与える	(過去形 gave)
H	hard	一生懸命に	
I	important	重要な、大切な	
L	lesson(s)	レッスン、けいこ	
	live	住む	(過去形 lived)
	look at …	…を見る	(過去形 looked at)
M	move	動く、身動きする	(過去形 moved)
N	now	ね、さて	
O	once upon a time	むかしむかし	
P	practice	練習する	(過去形 practiced)
R	repeat	くり返す (過去形 repeated) *repeat after ~ :* ～の後について言う	
	run away	逃げる	(過去形 ran away)
S	say	言う	(過去形 said)
	see	わかる	(過去形 saw)
	shout	叫ぶ	(過去形 shouted)
	(be) scared	こわがる、おびえる	
	(be) surprised	おどろく	
T	their	彼らの	
	think	考える	(過去形 thought)
	town	町 *in a small town :* 小さな町で	
	try to …	…してみる	(過去形 tried to)
	turn around	振り向く	(過去形 turned around)
V	voice	声 *in a big voice :* 大きな声で	
W	walk	散歩 *take a walk :* 散歩する	
	why	なぜ	
	with …	…といっしょに	

CD 1 🔊 英語をよく聞いて、それに合う絵の番号を選びましょう。

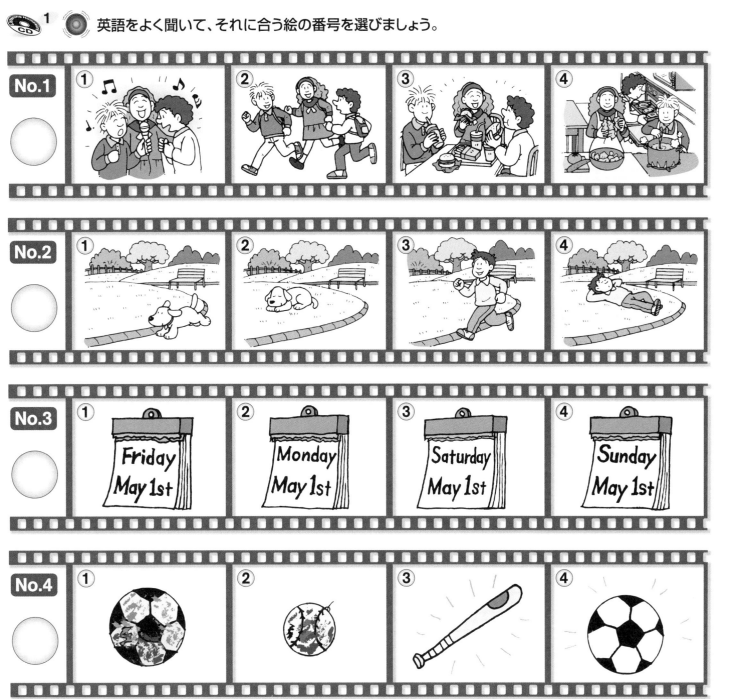

No.1 ○

No.2 ○

No.3 ① Friday May 1st ② Monday May 1st ③ Saturday May 1st ④ Sunday May 1st

No.4 ○

CD 2 🔊 4つの英文の中から、絵の内容を最もよく表している文の番号を選びましょう。

No.5 ( )

No.6 20歳 ( )

No.7 ( )

No.8 ( )

Listening Homework ②

  英語をよく聞いて、それに合う絵の番号を選びましょう。

No.1 ( )
 ①  ②  ③  ④

No.2 ( )
 ①  ②  ③  ④

No.3 ( )
 ①  ②  ③  ④

No.4 ( )
 ①  ②  ③  ④

 4つの英文の中から、絵の内容を最もよく表している文の番号を選びましょう。

No.5

( )

No.6

( )

No.7

( )

No.8

( )

5 次の絵について質問します。その答えとして最も適切なものの番号を選びましょう。

No.1

○

① It is sleeping. ② It is running.

③ It is skiing. ④ It is sunny.

No.2

○

① It is winter. ② It is sunny.

③ It is rainy. ④ It is windy.

No.3

○

① Two. ② One.

③ Three. ④ Four.

No.4

○

① He is sleeping. ② He is running.

③ He is skiing. ④ He is swimming.

6 4つの英文の中から、絵の内容を最もよく表している文の番号を選びましょう。

No.5	No.6	No.7	No.8
		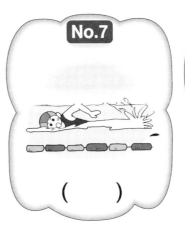	
( )	( )	( )	( )

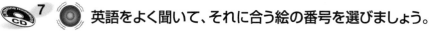

7 英語をよく聞いて、それに合う絵の番号を選びましょう。

No.1 ① ② ③ ④

No.2 ① Tadashi ② ③ ④

No.3 ① ② ③ ④

No.4 ① ② ③ ④

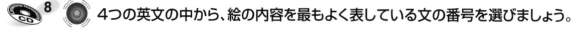

8 4つの英文の中から、絵の内容を最もよく表している文の番号を選びましょう。

No.5 ( )　No.6 ( )　No.7 ( )　No.8 ( )

9 次の絵について質問します。その答えとして最も適切なものの番号を選びましょう。

No.1
① Six people are sitting.   ② Four people are standing.
③ One woman is standing.   ④ Five people are sitting.

No.2
① It is sunny.   ② It is cloudy.
③ It is rainy.   ④ It is five o'clock.

No.3
① He is standing.   ② He is sleeping.
③ He is reading.   ④ He is cooking.

No.4
① In the airplane.   ② At home.
③ At school.   ④ In the train.

10 対話と質問を聞き、その答えとして最も適切なものの番号を選びましょう。

No.5
① Yes, she does.   ② She lives in Kanagawa.
③ She lives in Tokyo.   ④ No, she isn't.

No.6
① To the supermarket.   ② No, she doesn't.
③ She lives in the supermarket.   ④ With her mother.

No.7
① Yes, he does.   ② No, he doesn't.
③ He has two sisters.   ④ He is a brother.

No.8
① Yes, she is.   ② She has her homework.
③ She is doing her homework.   ④ No, she doesn't.

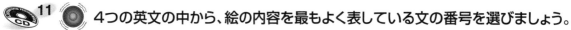

Listening Homework ❻

CD 11 🔘 4つの英文の中から、絵の内容を最もよく表している文の番号を選びましょう。

No.1	No.2	No.3	No.4
			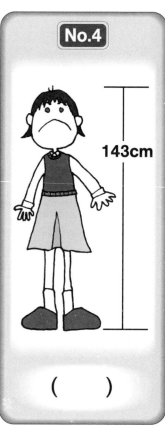
( )	( )	( )	( )

CD 12 🔘 対話と質問を聞き、その答えとして最も適切なものの番号を選びましょう。

No.5 ◯

① No, she can't.　② No, she isn't.

③ Yes, she does.　④ Yes, she can.

No.6 ◯

① She plays dodgeball.　② She plays baseball.

③ She plays tennis.　④ Yes, she does.

No.7 ◯

① In the living room.　② She is watching TV.

③ She is sleeping.　④ Yes, she does.

No.8 ◯

① No, he doesn't.　② I like hamburgers.

③ It is a hamburger.　④ Yes, he does.

13 次の絵について質問します。その答えとして最も適切なものの番号を選びましょう。

No.1
① It is sleeping. ② It is under the chair.
③ It is on the bed. ④ It is sitting.

No.2
① He is hungry. ② Yes, he is.
③ He is cooking dinner. ④ That is his dinner.

No.3
① She is sitting in the wheelchair. ② She is walking.
③ She is sick. ④ She is reading.

No.4
① There is a table. ② It is sleeping.
③ Yes, it is. ④ In the kitchen.

  14 対話と質問を聞き、その答えとして最も適切なものの番号を選びましょう。

No.5
① No, I don't. ② He likes math.
③ He likes P.E. ④ No, he doesn't.

No.6
① He has to play baseball. ② He has to go to the dentist.
③ He has to stay at home. ④ He has to go to school.

No.7
① Her birthday is January 29th. ② Her birthday is January 28th.
③ Her birthday is January 30th. ④ Her birthday is June 29th.

No.8
① By ferry. ② Last Sunday.
③ Victoria. ④ Yes, he did.

Listening Homework ❽

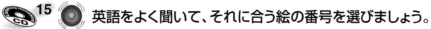

15 英語をよく聞いて、それに合う絵の番号を選びましょう。

No.1 ① ② ③ ④

No.2 ① ② ③ ④

No.3 ① ② ③ ④

No.4 ① ② ③ ④

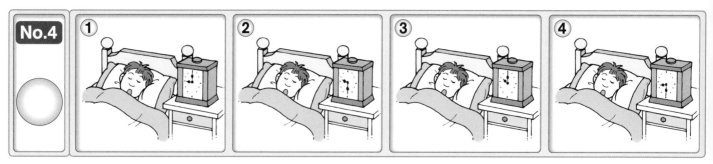

16 4つの英文の中から、絵の内容を最もよく表している文の番号を選びましょう。

No.5	No.6	No.7	No.8
( )	( )	( )	( )

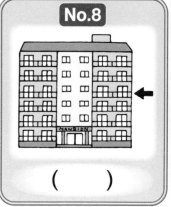

Listening Homework ❾

CD 17 ◉ イラストを参考にしながら、その答えとして最も適切なものの番号を選びましょう。

No.1
◯
① Yes, he is.
② He is a teacher.
③ His name is Taku.

No.2
◯
① It's on the chair.
② I can read.
③ I live in Nagasaki.

No.3
◯
① Me, too.
② After dinner.
③ I like English.

No.4
◯
① No, you can't.
② My name is Mary.
③ This is Mary speaking.

CD 18 ◉ 対話と質問を聞き、その答えとして最も適切なものの番号を選びましょう。

No.5
◯
① On Sundays.
② On Mondays.
③ On Wednesdays.
④ On Fridays.

No.6
◯
① Something to drink.
② Something to wear.
③ Something to read.
④ Something to eat.

No.7
◯
① Yes, he can.
② No, he can't.
③ He lives in England.
④ I can speak English well.

No.8
◯
① at six thirty
② go to bed
③ at six o'clock
④ really

19 イラストを参考にしながら、英語の質問に対して最も適切なものの番号を選びましょう。

No.1
1. I live in Fukuoka.
2. He lives in Fukuoka.
3. He is forty years old.

No.2
1. It's sunny.
2. By bus.
3. To the post office.

No.3
1. Her name is Yasuko.
2. Yes, but just a little.
3. She is fine, thank you.

No.4
1. He likes orange juice.
2. My brother is.
3. Your brother is.

  20 4つの英文の中から、絵の内容を最もよく表している文の番号を選びましょう。

No.5	No.6	No.7	No.8

(　　)	(　　)	(　　)	(　　)

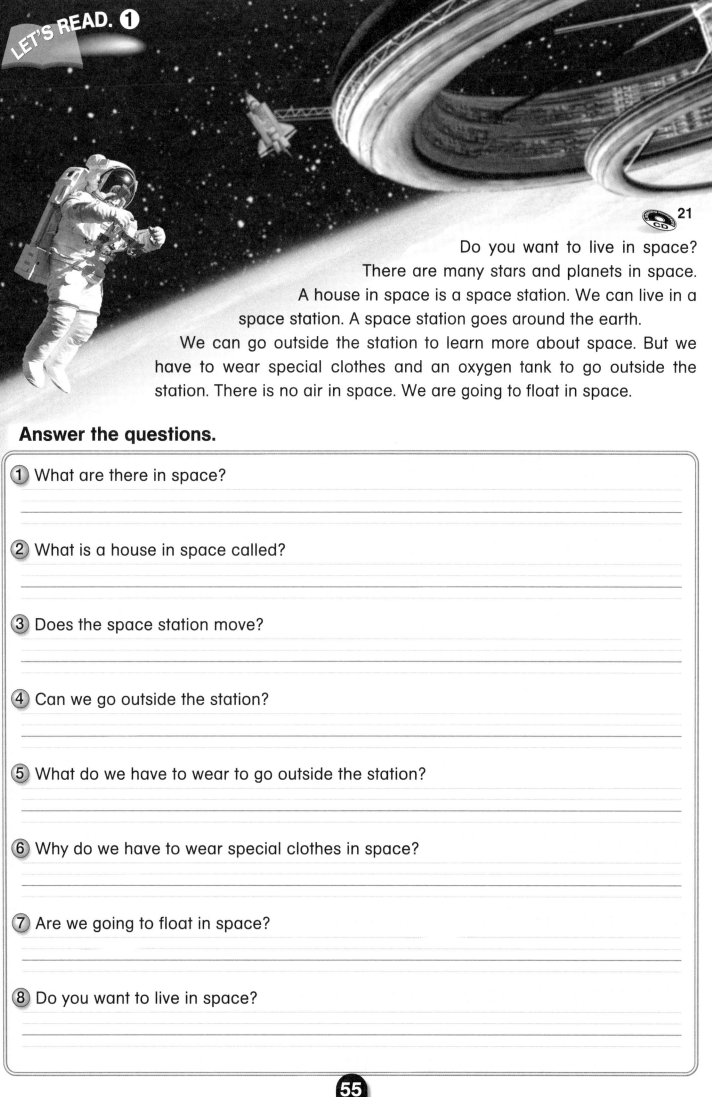

CD 21

Do you want to live in space?
There are many stars and planets in space.
A house in space is a space station. We can live in a
space station. A space station goes around the earth.
We can go outside the station to learn more about space. But we
have to wear special clothes and an oxygen tank to go outside the
station. There is no air in space. We are going to float in space.

Answer the questions.

① What are there in space?

② What is a house in space called?

③ Does the space station move?

④ Can we go outside the station?

⑤ What do we have to wear to go outside the station?

⑥ Why do we have to wear special clothes in space?

⑦ Are we going to float in space?

⑧ Do you want to live in space?

🔘 22

Did you ever see an ostrich? An ostrich is a big bird. It is very tall. It is sometimes nine feet tall. It has long legs and a long neck. It runs fast. But it can't fly. It is too big to fly. Most birds have four toes. An ostrich has only two toes. It can live to be seventy years old. The eggs of ostriches are very big. Ostriches live in Africa.

Answer the questions.

① What is an ostrich? _____

② Is an ostrich tall or short? _____

③ How tall is an ostrich?
_____
_____

④ Are the legs long? _____

⑤ Is the neck long? _____

⑥ Can an ostrich fly? _____

⑦ Why not? _____

⑧ How many toes do most birds have?
_____
_____

⑨ How many toes does an ostrich have?
_____
_____

⑩ How old can an ostrich live to be?
_____
_____

⑪ Are the eggs big? _____

⑫ Where do ostriches live? _____